Mindplay

Mastering the Art of Perception through Neuro-Linguistic Programming

Rex Morton

Copyright Page

Disclaimer

This book is intended to provide information about the fields of Neuro-Linguistic Programming (NLP) and Cognitive Behavioural Therapy (CBT) and their potential integration. While the author has made every effort to ensure that the information was correct at the time of publication, the author does not assume and hereby disclaims any liability to any party for any loss, damage, or disruption caused by errors or omissions, whether such errors or omissions result from negligence, accident, or any other cause.

The contents of this book should not be used as a substitute for professional advice, diagnosis, or treatment. The reader should always consult with a qualified healthcare provider about any mental health concerns or conditions. Never disregard professional psychological or medical advice or delay in seeking it because of something you have read in this book.

The views expressed in this work are solely those of the author and do not necessarily reflect the views of the publisher, and the publisher hereby disclaims any responsibility for them.

The inclusion of websites, links, or references to other resources does not mean that the author or the publisher endorses the information the organization or website may provide or recommendations it might make. Furthermore, the author does not guarantee the accuracy of the information these resources provide.

The use of any information provided in this book is solely at your own risk.

Chapter 1: Navigating the Mind's Language: An Introduction to Neuro-Linguistic Programming and Personal Branding

Welcome to a Journey of Self-Discovery and Influence

Imagine you could unlock the secret language of your mind, enabling you to understand yourself and others better, influence perceptions, and build a powerful personal brand. This is the world of Neuro-Linguistic Programming (NLP) - a fascinating realm where psychology, communication, and personal development converge.

Unraveling the Mysteries of NLP

Neuro-Linguistic Programming sounds like a complex term, but it's simply about understanding how we think (Neuro), communicate (Linguistic), and behave (Programming). NLP explores how our thoughts and words shape our reality and how we can tweak them for better outcomes.

The Core Principles of NLP:

The Map is Not the Territory: Our perception of the world is not the world itself but our interpretation of it.

Mind-Body Connection: Our thoughts, feelings, and physical actions are deeply interconnected.

The Ability to Choose: We possess the ability to select how we react and mold our experiences.The Rising Importance of Personal Branding

In today's digital age, where everyone is connected and information travels at lightning speed, how we present ourselves to the world matters more than ever. Personal branding isn't just for celebrities; it's for everyone. It's about how we want others to see and remember us, whether in person, online, or through our work.

Why Personal Branding Matters:

First Impressions Count: In our fast-paced world, first impressions can be lasting.

Digital Footprint: Our online presence tells a story about us - make sure it's the one you want to tell.

Career and Opportunities: A strong personal brand can open doors to new opportunities.

Transforming Personal Branding with NLP

NLP offers tools and techniques to enhance your personal brand. By understanding how we communicate and how others perceive us, we can shape our brand more effectively.

How NLP Elevates Personal Branding:

Self-Awareness: Gain clarity on your strengths, values, and what you want your brand to represent.

Effective Communication: Learn to use language that resonates with your audience, building rapport and trust.

Behavioral Flexibility: Adapt your approach to connect with different people in various contexts.

In Conclusion: Your Personal Branding Journey Begins

As you embark on this journey, remember that NLP is not about manipulation but about understanding and genuine connection. It's a tool for self-improvement and positive influence. So, let's dive into the exciting world of NLP and personal branding, where every word, thought, and action can bring you closer to the personal and professional image you aspire to create.

Reflection and Action:

Think About Your Brand: What three words would you like people to associate with you?

Observe Your Communication: How do you usually communicate with others? Are there patterns you'd like to change?

By exploring these concepts, you will begin to master the art of perception and influence, shaping your personal brand to reflect the best version of yourself.

Chapter 2: Building Your Brand: NLP Foundations for Personal Empowerment

Welcome to the Building Blocks of Your Brand Journey

This chapter is about setting a strong foundation for your personal brand using Neuro-Linguistic Programming (NLP). Think of NLP as your toolkit for understanding and shaping how you and others think and feel. Let's explore these tools and learn how to use them for personal branding.

Exploring the Basics of NLP

NLP is like learning the user manual for your brain. It's about understanding how we process experiences and how we can change our thoughts and actions for the better.

Key Concepts of NLP:

Representation Systems: We experience the world through our senses (seeing, hearing, feeling, tasting, and smelling). NLP teaches us to be aware of which sense we use the most and how to communicate effectively using all senses.

Anchoring: This is about creating a trigger for a specific emotional state. For example, thinking of a happy memory when you're feeling down.

Rapport: This is the art of building trust and understanding with others, essential for effective communication.

Understanding the Psychology of Perception and Influence

How we perceive ourselves and how others perceive us can be quite different. NLP helps bridge this gap by teaching us to understand and influence perceptions in a positive way.

Influencing Perceptions:

Empathy: Put yourself in someone else's shoes to understand their perspective.

Positive Language: Use words that create a positive image and avoid negative language.

Body Language: Non-verbal cues like gestures and posture speak volumes.

Techniques for Self-Awareness and Personal Development

Self-awareness is key in personal branding. NLP offers techniques to understand ourselves better and develop in areas we want to improve.

Reframing: Change how you view a situation to see the positive side or a new opportunity.

Goal Setting: Be clear about what you want to achieve and set specific, achievable goals.

Visualisation: Imagine your ideal self and situation vividly to help make it a reality.

In Conclusion: Laying the Groundwork for a Strong Personal Brand

By understanding these NLP basics, you're well on your way to developing a personal brand that truly represents you. Remember, Authenticity and consistency are key components of personal branding, and NLP gives you the means to accomplish both.

Reflection and Action:

Self-Reflection: What are your core values and strengths? How do these reflect in your personal brand?

Practice Empathy: Try to understand a recent conversation from the other person's perspective.

As you incorporate these NLP foundations into your life, you'll find your personal brand becoming more coherent and influential, reflecting the unique individual you are.

Chapter 3: Sculpting Your Story: NLP Techniques for Crafting Your Personal Brand

Welcome to the Art of Personal Brand Crafting

Imagine your personal brand as a sculpture you're shaping. It's a representation of who you are and what you stand for. In this chapter, we'll use Neuro-Linguistic Programming (NLP) techniques to help you mold and refine this sculpture, making your personal brand both authentic and influential.

Identifying and Shaping Your Personal Brand

Your personal brand is more than just a catchy tagline or a slick logo. It's the essence of your personality, values, and abilities.

How to Identify Your Personal Brand:

Self-Reflection: Think about what makes you unique. What are your strengths, passions, and values?

Feedback: Ask friends, family, and colleagues what words they would use to describe you.

Vision: Envision how you want to be perceived. What do you want people to think of when they hear your name?

Utilizing NLP Strategies to Enhance Brand Messaging

NLP can help make your communication more impactful, ensuring your brand message resonates with your audience.

Enhancing Your Message with NLP:

Mirroring: Adapt your communication style to match your audience, creating a sense of familiarity and trust.

Positive Language: Use words that evoke positive emotions and paint a picture of your brand.

Storytelling: Share stories that illustrate your values and skills, making your brand memorable.

Creating an Authentic and Powerful Personal Narrative

Your personal narrative is the story you tell about yourself. It's a blend of who you are, what you've done, and where you're going.
Crafting Your Narrative:

Authenticity: Be true to yourself. Your personal narrative should be a genuine reflection of who you are.

Coherence: Ensure your story is consistent across all platforms, from your social media profiles to your in-person interactions.

Inspiration: Your story should inspire and engage your audience, leaving them wanting to know more about you.

In Conclusion: Your Personal Brand as a Masterpiece

Crafting your personal brand is a journey of self-discovery and expression. By using NLP techniques, you can ensure that your brand is not only a true reflection of who you are but also resonates deeply with your audience.

Reflection and Action:

Write Your Story: Draft a short narrative about yourself, highlighting key moments that shaped you.

Test Your Brand: Share your narrative with a trusted friend or mentor and ask for feedback.

Your personal brand, shaped with the help of NLP, is not just how the world sees you, but also how you see yourself. It's a powerful tool for growth, opportunity, and connection.

Chapter 4: The Power of Words: Mastering Communication with NLP

Welcome to the World of Influential Communication

Communication is an art and a science. It's about more than just what we say; it's about how we say it and how it's received. In this chapter, we'll explore how Neuro-Linguistic Programming (NLP) can help you become a master communicator, enhancing your ability to influence, build trust, and shape perceptions effectively.

Advanced Language Patterns for Effective Communication

Effective communication is key to conveying your message clearly and persuasively. NLP offers techniques to refine your language and make your communication more impactful.

Enhancing Your Language Skills:

Precision: Use clear, specific language that leaves little room for misunderstanding.

Metaphors and Similes: These are powerful tools for making complex ideas relatable and memorable.

Sensory-Based Language: Engage your audience's senses (sight, sound, touch) in your descriptions to create a vivid and engaging narrative.

Influencing Public Perception through Language and Behavior

The way you communicate and behave greatly influences how others perceive you. NLP can help you align your language and actions with the image you want to project.

Shaping Perceptions:

Consistency: Ensure your words and actions are in harmony. This builds credibility and trust.

Positive Framing: Focus on the positive aspects of your message, even when addressing challenges.

Active Listening: Show genuine interest in others' perspectives, fostering respect and understanding.

Building Rapport and Trust with Your Audience

Rapport is the bond of trust and understanding you create with others. It's essential for effective communication and long-lasting relationships.

Creating a Connection:

Mirroring: Subtly match your communication style, body language, and tone with your audience to create a sense of familiarity and comfort.

Empathy: Demonstrate understanding and care for others' feelings and perspectives.

Authenticity: Be genuine in your interactions. Authenticity is key to building lasting trust.

In Conclusion: Communicating with Impact and Integrity

Mastering communication with NLP is about more than just speaking well; it's about connecting with others on a deeper level, understanding their needs, and expressing yourself authentically.

Reflection and Action:

Practice Active Listening: In your next conversation, focus fully on the other person, showing empathy and understanding.

Observe Language Use: Pay attention to how people respond to different words and phrases you use. What works best?

By applying these NLP techniques, you'll not only improve your communication skills but also enhance your personal and professional relationships, making your interactions more meaningful and impactful.

Chapter 5: Digital Impressions: NLP Techniques for Online Branding

Welcome to the Digital Stage of Your Personal Brand

In the digital world, your online presence is often the first impression people have of you. It's crucial to make this impression count. This chapter will guide you on how to use Neuro-Linguistic Programming (NLP) techniques to enhance your digital footprint and ensure consistency in your online branding.

Leveraging NLP in Digital Communications

The principles of NLP can be incredibly effective in the digital realm, where communication is often text-based and lacks non-verbal cues.

Adapting NLP for Digital Use:

Clear and Engaging Language: Use language that is easy to understand and engages the reader right away.

Tone Matching: Mirror the tone of your audience in your online communications to create rapport.

Positive Framing: Even in writing, focus on positive language to convey optimism and confidence.

Enhancing Online Presence with NLP Techniques

Your online presence is a mosaic of everything you post, share, and comment on. NLP can help you curate this presence to reflect your personal brand accurately.

Strategies for a Strong Online Presence:

Consistent Messaging: Ensure that your online posts align with your personal brand and the image you want to project.

Engagement: Use language that invites interaction and creates a sense of community.

Storytelling: Share stories and experiences that reflect your values and mission.

Managing Social Media Interactions for Brand Consistency

Social media is a powerful tool for personal branding, but it requires careful management to maintain brand consistency.

Keeping Your Brand Consistent on Social Media:

Regular Audits: Periodically review your social media profiles and posts to ensure they align with your brand.

Responsive Communication: Engage with your audience in a way that reinforces your brand values and message.

Adaptable Approach: Be ready to adapt your strategy in response to feedback and changing trends.

In Conclusion: Your Digital Brand as a Reflection of You

Remember, your online brand is an extension of yourself. By applying NLP techniques to your digital communications, you can create a compelling and consistent online presence that truly represents who you are.

Reflection and Action:

Review Your Digital Presence: Look through your social media profiles and posts. Do they align with how you want to be perceived?

Engage with Purpose: In your next online interaction, focus on creating engagement that reflects your personal brand values.

As you refine your digital footprint with these NLP techniques, you'll find yourself building a stronger, more coherent online presence that resonates with your audience and reflects your authentic self.

Chapter 6: Turning Challenges into Opportunities: Overcoming Adversity with NLP

Welcome to the Resilient Side of Personal Branding

Facing challenges and negative perceptions is a part of life, especially when you're in the public eye. This chapter will guide you through using Neuro-Linguistic Programming (NLP) techniques to navigate criticism, rebrand effectively, and maintain a resilient, positive mindset.

Dealing with Criticism and Negative Feedback Using NLP

Criticism can be tough, but it's also an opportunity for growth. NLP offers tools to help you process feedback constructively.

Handling Criticism Gracefully:

Reframing: View criticism as a chance to learn and improve. Shift your perspective from defensive to curious.

Separating Fact from Opinion: Distinguish between constructive feedback and mere opinion or negativity.

Empathetic Response: Understand where the criticism is coming from and respond with empathy, not hostility.

Rebranding and Changing Public Perception

Sometimes, your personal brand needs a refresh. Maybe your goals have changed, or you're overcoming a setback. NLP can assist in this transformation.

Effective Rebranding Strategies:

Clear Vision: Define what you want your new brand to represent. Be specific and intentional.

Consistent Messaging: Communicate your new brand clearly across all platforms.

Positive Associations: Use language and imagery that create positive associations with your new brand.

Strategies for Maintaining Resilience and a Positive Mindset

Resilience is key in personal branding. It's about bouncing back stronger from setbacks and maintaining a positive outlook.

Building Resilience:

Positive Affirmations: Use positive statements about yourself and your abilities to boost confidence.

Visualization: Envision yourself accomplishing your objectives and triumphantly conquering obstacles.

Self-Care: Take care of your physical and mental well-being. A healthy mind and body are crucial for resilience.

In Conclusion: Embracing Change and Growth

Overcoming challenges and negative perceptions is not just about dealing with the immediate issue. It's about growing stronger and more adaptable. With NLP, you can turn these experiences into stepping stones for personal and brand growth.

Reflection and Action:

Reflect on Feedback: Think about recent criticism you've received. How can you use it constructively?

Practice Resilience: Next time you face a challenge, use positive affirmations and visualization to maintain a positive mindset.

By applying these NLP techniques, you will not only navigate through tough times more smoothly but also emerge with a stronger, more resilient personal brand.

Chapter 7: Crafting Your Narrative: The Magic of Storytelling in Branding

Welcome to the World of Storytelling

Every brand has a story, and how you tell that story can make all the difference. This chapter explores the art of storytelling in branding, showing you how to weave your personal or business narrative in a way that captivates, influences, and remains memorable.

Harnessing the Art of Storytelling to Captivate and Influence

Storytelling is not just about relaying facts; it's about engaging emotions and imagination. It's a powerful tool to connect with your audience on a deeper level.

Engaging Through Stories:

Emotional Connection: Stories that evoke emotions create a stronger bond with your audience.

Relatability: Share experiences that your audience can relate to, making your brand more accessible.

Authenticity: Be genuine in your storytelling. Authentic stories resonate more deeply with people.

Structuring Your Story with NLP Methods

NLP provides a framework to structure your story in a way that is both engaging and effective.

Creating a Compelling Narrative:

Setting the Scene: Start by setting the context. Give your audience a sense of place and time.

Developing the Plot: Introduce a challenge or a turning point. This is where the story gets interesting.

Resolution: Conclude with how you overcame the challenge or what you learned from the experience.

Making Your Brand Story Memorable and Impactful

A great story is one that sticks with your audience long after they've heard it. Using NLP techniques, you can make your brand story both memorable and impactful.

Ensuring Your Story Stands Out:

Sensory Details: Use descriptive language to create vivid mental images.

Repetition and Rhythm: Repeat key phrases or concepts to create a rhythm that's easy to follow.

Call to Action: End your story with a call to action, guiding your audience on what to do next.

In Conclusion: Your Story, Your Brand

The stories you tell form the backbone of your personal brand. They are the medium through which people connect with you and remember you. By harnessing the power of storytelling and structuring your narrative with NLP techniques, you can create a brand story that is not only engaging but also leaves a lasting impact.

Reflection and Action:

Craft Your Story: Write down your personal or brand story. Use the structure outlined to shape your narrative.

Share and Refine: Share your story with friends or colleagues. Gather feedback and refine your story for greater impact.

Remember, your brand story is more than just words; it's an experience you share with your audience. Make it count!

Chapter 8: Learning from the Best: Success Stories in NLP-Enhanced Branding

Welcome to the Gallery of Inspiration

In this chapter, we'll explore real-life examples of individuals who have successfully used Neuro-Linguistic Programming (NLP) techniques to build and enhance their personal brands. By analyzing their strategies and the lessons learned, we can gain valuable insights to apply in our own branding journeys.

Hypothetical Case Study 1: The Transformational Coach

Background:

A life coach who struggled with self-promotion and connecting with potential clients.

Application of NLP:

Rapport Building: Implemented NLP techniques to establish trust and understanding during interactions.

Positive Language: Used positive, empowering language in marketing materials and social media.

Goal Visualization: Regularly visualized achieving business goals to maintain motivation and focus.

Outcome:

Increased client base due to improved communication and a more engaging online presence.

Developed a strong, trust-based relationship with clients.

Lesson Learned:

Effective communication and positive language are key in building trust and rapport with your audience.

Hypothetical Case Study 2: The Entrepreneur

Background:

An entrepreneur who faced challenges in articulating their unique selling proposition.

Application of NLP:

Storytelling: Crafted a compelling brand story that highlighted personal experiences and business journey.

Sensory Language: Used vivid, sensory language in storytelling to create a more immersive experience.

Anchoring: Associated positive emotions with the brand through consistent imagery and messaging.

Outcome:

Established a unique and memorable brand identity.

Enhanced customer engagement and loyalty.

Lesson Learned:

A well-crafted story can powerfully convey your brand's essence and values.

Hypothetical Case Study 3: The Public Speaker

Background:

A public speaker who wanted to enhance stage presence and audience connection.

Application of NLP:

Mirroring: Adjusted body language and tone to mirror the audience, creating a sense of empathy.

Reframing: Turned stage anxiety into excitement and opportunity for engagement.

Feedback Loop: Used audience feedback to refine and adapt presentations for better impact.

Outcome:

Improved audience engagement and positive reviews.

Increased demand for speaking engagements.

Lesson Learned:

Adapting to and learning from your audience's feedback can significantly improve your brand presence.

In Conclusion: The Power of Real-World Examples

These case studies demonstrate the versatility and effectiveness of NLP in various contexts of personal branding. From coaches to entrepreneurs to public speakers, the principles of NLP can be adapted to suit different needs and goals.

Reflection and Action:

Identify Your Needs: Which aspects of NLP could most benefit your personal brand?

Action Plan: Develop a plan to integrate these NLP techniques into your branding strategy.

Remember, the journey of personal branding is unique to each individual. Take inspiration from these success stories, and forge your own path to branding excellence.

Chapter 9: Navigating Tomorrow: The Future of Personal Branding and NLP

Welcome to the Frontier of Branding and Communication

As we look to the future, it's essential to stay ahead of the curve in personal branding and NLP. This chapter explores emerging trends and prepares you for the evolving digital landscape, emphasizing the importance of continuous learning and adaptation.

Emerging Trends in NLP and Branding

The world of NLP and branding is constantly evolving, with new trends and technologies shaping the way we communicate and present ourselves.

Key Future Trends:

Technology Integration: Advances in AI and machine learning are expected to offer new ways to analyze and improve communication patterns.

Personalization: As audiences crave more personalized experiences, NLP can help tailor messages to individual preferences and needs.

Emotional Intelligence: There's a growing focus on understanding and responding to emotional cues in communication, both in-person and online.

Preparing for Future Changes in the Digital Landscape

The digital world is dynamic, and staying adaptable is key to maintaining a strong personal brand.

Adapting to Digital Changes:

Stay Informed: Keep up with the latest digital trends and tools. This could be through online courses, webinars, or industry news.

Flexibility: Be ready to adjust your strategies in response to new platforms and changes in audience behavior.

Digital Ethics: As digital interactions increase, being mindful of privacy and ethical considerations will be crucial.

Continuous Learning and Adaptation in NLP and Branding

The only constant in life is change, and this is especially true for NLP and branding. Continuous learning is essential.

Embracing Lifelong Learning:

Ongoing Education: Regularly update your NLP knowledge and skills through workshops, courses, or self-study.

Feedback Loops: Actively seek feedback on your communication and branding efforts and use it for improvement.

Experimentation: Don't be afraid to try new approaches. Innovation is key to staying relevant.

In Conclusion: Staying Ahead in a Changing World

The future of personal branding and NLP is exciting and filled with opportunities. By staying informed, adaptable, and committed to continuous learning, you can ensure that your personal brand remains strong and relevant in the years to come.

Reflection and Action:

Future-Proofing Plan: Develop a plan to regularly update your skills and knowledge in NLP and digital branding.

Experiment: Try out a new digital tool or platform and observe its impact on your branding efforts.

As you embark on this ongoing journey, remember that the future belongs to those who are prepared to learn, adapt, and innovate. Your personal brand is your story to tell – make it a compelling one, today and tomorrow.

Chapter 10: Bringing It All Together: Integrating NLP into Your Personal Branding Journey

Welcome to the Culmination of Your NLP and Branding Adventure

This final chapter is a celebration of what you've learned and a guide to moving forward. Let's recap the key lessons and strategies from this journey and develop a personal action plan to integrate NLP into your personal branding.

Recap of Key Lessons and Strategies

Throughout this book, we've explored the powerful combination of Neuro-Linguistic Programming and personal branding. Here's a brief reminder of the key points:

Understanding Yourself and Others: NLP helps in understanding the nuances of communication and perception.

Effective Communication: We've seen how NLP can enhance how we communicate, both online and in-person.

Adapting to Change: The importance of being adaptable and responsive to feedback in shaping your personal brand.

Storytelling: The power of storytelling in creating an engaging and memorable personal brand.

Resilience: Strategies for dealing with challenges and maintaining a positive, resilient mindset.

Developing a Personal Action Plan

To effectively integrate NLP into your personal branding journey, it's crucial to have a plan. Here's a simple framework to get started:

Set Clear Goals: What do you want to achieve with your personal brand? Be specific.

Identify NLP Techniques: Choose which NLP strategies align best with your goals.

Implement and Practice: Start applying these techniques in your daily communication.

Regular Review: Periodically review your progress and adjust your strategies as needed.

Final Thoughts and Encouragement for the Reader

As you embark on this exciting journey, remember that personal branding is not a one-time task but an ongoing process of growth and evolution. It's about telling your story, your way.

In Conclusion: Your Journey Continues

Integrating NLP into your personal branding is a journey of self-discovery, learning, and growth. It's about finding your unique voice and using it to connect with the world authentically and effectively.

Reflection and Action:

Your First Step: Identify one NLP technique you found most intriguing and apply it this week in a small way.

Long-Term Vision: Write down where you see your personal brand in one year. Use this vision to guide your actions.

Remember, every great journey begins with a single step. Your personal branding adventure, powered by NLP, is yours to explore and enjoy. Here's to your success and the amazing brand you're about to build!

About the Author

Rex Morton is a renowned author and researcher in the United Kingdom with a passionate interest in the human mind, specifically in Cognitive Behavioural Therapy (CBT) and Neuro-Linguistic Programming (NLP).

Morton has spent a considerable portion of his professional life diving deep into the theories and principles that form the backbone of these two compelling fields. His fascination with NLP led him to complete an extensive certification program, solidifying his understanding of this innovative approach to understanding human behaviour.

Although Morton does not have clinical experience, his intense curiosity and dedication to studying these subjects have made him a respected figure in the field. He has thoroughly researched the integration of NLP techniques into CBT, offering fresh perspectives and insights into how these two methodologies can complement each other to enhance understanding of human cognition and behaviour.

As an author, Morton has successfully communicated his knowledge and passion to a broader audience, making complex psychological theories accessible to professionals and interested laypersons. His writing is characterized by a clear, engaging style and a focus on the practical application of theories, making them relevant to everyday life.

In his personal life, Morton is an ardent lover of the natural world, often spending his free time exploring the British countryside. His passion for landscape photography allows him to capture and share the beauty of these excursions. Despite his accomplishments, Morton is known for his humility and eagerness to continue learning. His work continues to inspire those interested in the intricate workings of the human mind and the exciting possibilities presented by the integration of NLP and CBT.

Join the Journey at RexMorton.com

If you've found the content of this book enlightening and wish to continue your journey of understanding the human mind, I warmly invite you to visit my website at www.rexmorton.com. The website serves as a hub of knowledge where I share my latest findings, thoughts, and insights on the integration of NLP and CBT.

I also encourage you to subscribe to the newsletter available on the website. By subscribing, you'll receive regular updates on a range of topics, from detailed discussions on specific NLP techniques and their application in CBT, to the latest research in the field.

The newsletter is also the first place I'll share news of upcoming releases. Whether it's the announcement of a new book, the launch of an online course, newsletter subscribers will be the first to know. This is a great opportunity to continue learning directly from me, deepening your understanding of NLP and CBT, and enhancing your skills in applying these techniques in your own life or professional practice.

I'm looking forward to sharing this journey with you.